POWER OF PRAISE
Poetry of Spiritual Christianity

by Branch Isole

Copyright © 2005

Power of Praise
Poetry of Spiritual Christianity ™
by Branch Isole

Printed in the United States of America

Library of Congress Control Number:
2004114729
ISBN 0-9747692-7-4

PO Box 1696
Lahaina, HI 96767-1696

Additional copies available at:
www.manaopublishing.com
or www.fellowship-of-believers.com

"And being in anguish, he prayed more earnestly and his sweat was like drops of blood falling to the ground."

~Luke 22:44

Contents

On My Knees
Overweight
Parousia Timetable
Passion Soliloquy
Patrician Prayer
Penance
Pilot
Poison
Printed in Red
Reclamation
Religiosity
Requiem Nails
Rewards
See Saw
State of Being
Stewardship
Stream of Consciousness
Tempered Temptations
The Box
The Way
The Word
Up In Smoke
Waiting Game
Within, Without
Worlds
Worship Questions

Introduction

God's Love.
One of the great struggles for the Christian is
the double edge sword of discipleship. With the
eventual realization and therefore necessary
acceptance to follow Jesus Christ, belief slowly
becomes a prerequisite response of everyday
action and not merely a one-time conversion
of understanding.

Having surrendered with enlightened intentions
to faithfully emulate Christ, many believers may
discover the trials and tribulations in their lives
increasing with exacerbated intensity and/or
frequency.

Two reasons this may occur are: First, the
forces of evil in the world do not wish to lose
even one soul to the discipleship of Jesus Christ.
If you are familiar with the Bible then you're
aware that Satan already knows how the story
ends. The devil knows the will of God better
than any man or woman alive and he is
cognizant of his destiny. With this knowledge,
his sole mission is to take with him into the
depths of the abyss and to separate from God as
many souls as possible.

The second reason is as much a part of God's plan for each of us, as is His allowance of the force of evil itself. It is found in His providential granting of our 'free will' to choose and decide our own spiritual fate. God waits patiently to discover if our behavioral responses of repentance will finally take root in our hearts with each revised penitent commitment we make.

Will we exhibit our decision to come closer to Him through obedience to His word by 'staying the course' on a path of faithful belief? Or do we continue to ask for a momentary reprieve from the perils of our immediate troubles and then silently slip back into our daily existence of self?

Life is full of struggle and we each experience trouble and heartbreak. Jesus advised of this reality in His sermons and parable teachings while giving guidance and instruction as to our human condition. In the Gospels he proclaims "If anyone would come after me, he must deny himself, take up his cross daily and follow me." It is here we find the answer which many Christians miss, others search for, and most grapple with. True Christian belief and discipleship is grounded in the principle of daily denying of self and daily living in obedience to God's Word; through the examples, thoughts, words and deeds of Jesus the Christ.

A co-existence between the spiritual and the pragmatic is essential. Not only does God know and love each of us as we are, but more importantly He is waiting for each of us to know and accept Him for who He is.

This acknowledgment of God coupled with a new found understanding of His love and compassion encourages us to accept ourselves and discover His Son's examples of how we should live and treat each other. Jesus described this treatise on life in the biblical account of Matthew 22:37 when He instructs us to "Love the Lord your God with all your heart and with all your soul and with all your mind. . . and Love your neighbor as yourself."

There are none who are better in God's eyes, for each transgression against His holy instruction is unacceptable in his sight. When we come to realize and understand this, it frees us to look for and learn a different way to live; in obedience to Him and at peace with each other.

Branch Isole

If we get too moral
we may forget we are sinners.

~Henry David Thoreau

for Christopher John Gentile
1961-2008

Everyone who knew Chris genuinely liked him.

Ainokea

God's spoken words
in declaration of His universal sovereignty
for all to hear and understand
were contained in His statement
"I am who I am"

Satan,
that fallen angel
unable to take
God's Holy place
was cast to earth
to plague and lead astray
this whole human race

With temptations, deceit, lies
and sin
his job each day
souls to win
Gathering to his side
all who might into the abyss ride
that they may with him abide

Interesting isn't it
after all these years
the one who has caused
so many tears
Satan, that old deceiver
has a stronghold grasp
on so many believers

Satan has tried
to be as God from the start
and his success is in
playing man's heart
Twisting God's own sovereign words
"I am"

That's not however
what Satan declares
as he watches and waits
on man's despair

The devil is no fool
inviting many
to be drawn to him
and his evil ways
By planting seeds
within the common
woman or man
who truly think
it's all about them

You see it
over and over again
in our behavior
our actions
our irresponsibility
Multitudes worldwide
openly declare
"It's all about me"

How has Satan
circumvented his place
and condemned those of us
in this human race
who state daily a plethora
of our self purposed Ainokea?

God exclaimed
"I am, I am"
Satan has taught us
to proudly proclaim
"*It*'s *about me*"
"*It*'s *about me*"
(I am I am)

[Ainokea (pronounced Eye No Key Ah)
Hawaiian connotation for
'It's all about me'
literal meaning; "I do what I like"
"I do what I want"]

Birthing Partner

Visiting his birthing partner
one last time today
Dressed in her finest
she's finally gone away
Going home
he was told
Prepared for travel
brave and bold

Or was she?
He stared and wondered

Had she planned at all
for this day,
the day she'd be put
down and under

She never talked of it
Not to his knowledge,
not through grade school
high school or even college

Exclaimed she 'believed'
That was to be
her last word
on the 'Son of Man'
Now she'll be
finding out first hand

Bidding farewell
to his birthing partner
of oh so long ago
Until he too arrives postmortem
he will never know

Blessings

Learning early the fear
of discipline
Not from love
but from falling tears
Cowering back from possibilities
Afraid to go forward
stricken for years.

Again and again
opportunity knocked
Still doubt reigned
over actions and talk.

Sacrificed, on the front
Thrown to lions
and bullies in alleys
Young lives strapped and bound
shackled beneath
down in the galleys
To row ever bow-ward
while facing astern
Left to starve,
to rot and to burn.

Where is the grace
the saving face?
Where is the finish of this race?

Living vicariously
through his own seed
Remembering his longings
his failures
his need.
Waiting and waiting
day by day
As time slips slowly
then faster away
Frightened by his future
Running to,
or from his past
Caught between anticipation and regret
Surely, not the last.
Missing the moment
beating himself up
One more time
not nearly enough.

To be led astray
by those loved and trusted
To attempt one's own flight
from being used,
abused
scourged
and busted.

Broken bones, broken home
History repeating itself
Realizing finally
We each are alone.

Alone on our journey
from there to here
and perhaps,
even back again
Regaining our souls
Released from our sin.

Sins of the world
Sins of mankind
Actions of evil
continue to bind.

To bind us, to threaten us and finally for death
To be released once again for the ultimate test

Living vicariously
through her own seed
Sensing her longings
her failures
her need.
Waiting and waiting
day by day
As time slips slowly
then faster away
Frightened by her future,
Torn by her past
Caught between anticipation and regret
Surely not the last.
Missing the moment
beating herself up
One more time
not nearly enough.

Do we believe?
In whom
what and why?
Believe and smile at our final relief?
Or once more to try,
to cry. . .
and still wonder why?

Each coin has two sides
And so too the sword
So it is with life and death
For believer and non, of God's eternal Word.

Stretched pass the point of no return
this way or that,
to go on
or turn back?
Turn to where?
Which way?
What door?
The world waits and tempts
with its many whores.

Living vicariously
through our own seeds
Knowing our longings
our failures
our needs.
Waiting and waiting
day by day
As time slips slowly
then faster away

Frightened by our future
Tortured by our past
Caught between anticipation and regret
Surely not the last.
Missing the moment
beating ourselves up
One more time
Never enough.

We stumble, we fall
along the route
One moment elated
the next down and out.

Waiting on the meaning
of this bold life
Waiting to excise
with its cold knife.
Feeling the blade
made of steel
Buried deep,
falling to kneel
Cutting out of the heart
all its disease
Cutting out the sins
and finding release.

One life has ended
a new one begun
Finally,
wisdom and freedom to run.

His Blessing now given
and now understood
Not made of
stone
marble
or wood
The Blessing of Life;
Love,
one hundred proof

The Blessing received
revealed in the Truth.

Brothers in Arms

Brothers in form, in peace and in right
Brothers in life, in death from the fight
We would all be brothers in heart and in might
If only we loved each other
with His Holy Light.

Clouds

Oh clouds you are drawn
to the land
as a moth to the flame
Ever upward
higher and higher
Collecting together
producing the rain

Some billow
Some cirrus
Each on his own
all part of the sum
At long last
becoming as one

One white as snow
another so dark
gray in between
With thunderous voices do they hark
as if splitting
at the seams

Heralding your coming
your presence
your fall
At once full and mighty
At once not at all

To let down your essence
To spill out your rain
Giving life
to every plant
flower
and plain

This is your course
your being
your path
God has made you
that all else might last

For without your water
your moisture
your dew
None,
no
not one
would survive without you

Watching you race
across the sky
Bringing shade, cool breezes
a tear from an eye?
Or your sprinkle
from on high?

The life you bring
from day and night sky
From mist
to drizzle
to torrent,
With no more than a sigh

Here one moment
gone the next
As we below stare
and wonder perplexed
We love you, we hate you
Without you we lust
For us in this place
you are never enough
When you are with us
we know not why
When you are gone
we have need and do cry

Oh clouds,
full of love
up in the sky
Stroll as you must
Stroll as you will
From over the seas
up into the hills
Drawn by the heat
of land far below
Drawn ever onward
sliding up as you go
Full at once
and then again empty
Constant regeneration
you feed all aplenty

Oh clouds
you are drawn
as the moth to a flame
Forever providing
life giving rain

Waters that stream
from your vaporous demise
are from river of life
which flows from on high
From the throne of God
does all life proceed
From the hand of God
is fulfilled every need

Oh clouds
filled,
by your rain from within
So is it with us
filled with our sin

May we be cleansed
by the love of the Lord
The same as your rain
washes clean every shore

Comedian

Voltaire had it right
when he nailed your act
describing your audience "too afraid to laugh"
delivering one liners
because you can and so choose

tossing airborne your two sided coinage
watching it float, teetering on edge
false sense of endearment
fear of retribution, which will it be
our outstretched arms strain over the ledge

beat docile and frightened
fragility keeps us pegged
as pachyderm to the stump
we hold all the cards
lest one of course
yours, always, mega-trump

all this because you didn't want to be alone
all this to ensure throngs before your throne
you create
you plan
you design
each niche
why so often do your three monty efforts
appear as bait and switch

Coming Out

Is this the day,
the day I come out,
come out of the closet?

Is today the day,
the day I reveal to the world
I am and have been
for as long as I can remember
Homosexual,
Gay
Queer
Fag
Pansy
Dandy. . .
There, I've said it

What about you
Pharisaic Christian?
Is my speck so great
you can't see
your plank of hypocrisy,
Shall it just fade away?

Now to climb
the highest steeple
and openly declare
to every person
to all people

I'm out
I'm finally out
I haven't changed
I'm not deranged
It's still me
Let me be free

Free to live my life
To love who I am
and who I will
All I ask
is you let me choose,
just as I allow
you to do

What about you
Church Age Christian?
Is my speck so great
you can't see
your plank of dogma,
Shall it just fade away?

I'm aware of what the Bible says
Did *you* miss the part
where in His sight,
a sin is a sin

I'll let God be my judge
and put me in my place
when I see Him
face to face

What about you
Carnal Christian?
Is my speck so great
you can't see
your plank of self-righteousness,
Shall it just fade away?

Conflict

For the believing Christian
Jesus endures the wrath of one's past
Setting free the sinner
the transgressors, you and me
His claim
to serve
on the cross in our stead
A replacement for us
answering the call of death

same as we
his eternal soul became man
to experience our ways
our nature, understand
to catch more than a glimpse
of our self-centered indulgence

the difference between
he and we?
our spirit
tainted, stained
his spirit pure
this his reason
his choice to endure

the challenge for all
who have ever lived?
truly comprehend
the power of free will

for this the main difference
between we and he;
His spirit willing
our body weak

Cruel and Usual

Of all God's creatures
large and small
the cruelest by far
of them all
is the human child
at about age ten,
That is
of course
until he grows
to be a man
Then he can become
a true abuser,
a tyrant
and demonizer
of his own
children and women
and start the cycle
all over again

When the Bible instructs
as to seven generations
of admonishing woes,
it's not always
of plagues
and perils
and pain,

but of inappropriate
hateful
and unloving behavior
that flows,
from parent to child
and to subsequent offspring,
and so it goes
and so it goes

If you want to identify
this behavior for yourself
just look around
and you will see
the fruit doesn't fall
far from the tree

Once a child learns
what he or she sees
and experiences
first hand,
be it open or fist
or a twist of the wrist
out of anger
and anguish
of insecurity,
the pattern is set
into perpetuity

So if you observe it
ask someone involved
to be the adult
and put a stop to it all,
immediately

And if it is your own behavior
towards the ones
you so called 'love'
then seek aid
and assistance
from both here
and above

Break the cycle
of abuse
once and for all!
That both you
and your children
may again,
stand tall.

Deadly Sins

Proudly proclaiming
himself to be
a called man of God
His presentation that
of a charismatic bear
for he is enormously huggable,
like others
behind those vestments worn
his life too
a see-sawing struggle

His penchant;
money making schemes
ideas and thoughts abound
Built on the backs
of subservient others
those who are out and down
Believing him the way
in need of his, being around

A taste of the Word,
shelter,
essential needs be filled
but one of the roles
they acquiesce to
is that of recovering shill

His expectation in return
indentured service sans retreat
Masked as freedom
to help each of them
get back on their feet

Cars, trucks
expensive motorcycles,
to him they come and go
Passing through his hands;
houses, acreage, land
Material avarice veiled beneath
the banner of this Pied Piper's clan

Now I wouldn't really
call it sloth
it's more like too much stuff
When I asked him
why so much? His answer,
"when is enough enough?"

One of his flock
recently announced,
he has changed immensely
"He's more under control
a kinder, gentler fellow
whose anger has now subsided
For now if you decide
to take your leave
he won't kick you out
nor will you now be chided"

My wife happened to mention
his greeting hug one Sunday,
felt to her more than friendly
"to say the least" she said to me
"his rub
rubbed me the wrong way"

Now I'm not one to throw those stones
be they big or small
for the house I live in is full of glass
inhabited by a sinner
But our portions differ in comparison
for breakfast, lunch and dinner
for between the two of us
I admit, being somewhat thinner

He called me just the other day
an offer for me to take
Thanking him for thinking of me
heartily I declined
For his offers most often mean
a payday for him
at the expense of the offeree

He said he'd heard
that we'd done well
proceeding to say his good bye
But something in his parting tone
gave a sense he wished
we'd go to. . .

well, you know.

Differentials

there are His poems
and there are my poems
the difference plain to see
His are about truth and love
mine are about mine and me

Electrical Orchestration

Remove from me all matter Lord
all gas and liquid too
Leave only the electric charge
that was me originally, from You.

Take the soul and spirit aura
of these molecules
which were of and by,
and with You before

Since the beginning
when they were combined
in new form
from the myriad of possibilities
of all your worlds

Reconstitute them once more Lord
in a fashion of your choice
That the new me
might be, more like You

That the new charge
re-formed from your hands
this time,
might serve You
instead of myself.

Fellowship of Believers Prayer

God in heaven
Maker of all things
Judge of all men
I acknowledge and bewail
my manifold sins and wickedness
against thee and thy divine majesty
in thought, word and deed
Have mercy on my soul

Grant that I may here ever after
walk in newness of life
and follow the light of the world
my Lord and Savior
Jesus Christ

Lord come dwell in my heart
for you know what it is
I wish to do
and that is to serve you
this day and all the days of my life

For you are the master
and I am the servant
You are the vine
and I am the branch
You are the potter
and I am the clay
May I abide in you
that you would abide in me
May I serve you by serving others
and serve others while serving you

May your spirit guide me
lead me
and direct me
to where you would have me be
That all I am might reflect of you
and all I do
might be good works in your name
bringing honor and glory to you and the Father

These things I ask and pray
in the name of Jesus Christ
the true son
of the living God

my Lord
my Savior
my Rock
my Redeemer
my Fortress
my Shield
my Strength and my God.
Amen

First Rule of Correction

"Whack"
resonated the sound
of the wooden rule
hard, coming down
Breaking the silence
that hung in the air
like a mist
of sullen despair

Within a second
a collective gasp
raced audibly
through the room,
Another hand
had met its doom

Somewhere
in our austere chamber
decorated white
Another mate
had now, seen the light

No one moved
to say the least
For all had heard
the bellowing beast

Of all who heard
not one said, a single word
but all together
a mouthing choir
managed to whisper,
"yes, Sister"

"Silence is Golden
and I Want Some Gold!"
She shrieked out loud
as she stalked
and strutted
to the front of the crowd

No need to look
nor even to glance
no one dared peer
at the great, black and white bear

So familiar the sulk
of this habited hulk
All knew her sneer
permanently affixed there

One quickly learned
the fear and the dread
of daily confinement with she,
who seemed to have eyes
in the back of her head

Surely custom made
this flattened and measured
twelve inch blade
Perfect for punishing
each little bugger
Chip off the old block
from a Louisville slugger

Having experienced the trauma
of her unbridled wrath
which was channeled into
that appendage of ash
Wincing back
a single tear,
dripping to the page
like a drop of rain
Wondering whose hand
was now newly bludgeoned
Red with whelps
and searing pain

Recalling vividly
what little fun
was found at God's school
with the Sisterhood of Nuns
When I, was in grade one.

Gentle Breeze

Oh gentle breeze
How long has it been?
How far have you traveled?
The warmth of your being
brushes against my skin,
cooling the radiant air
which surrounds me.

You, oh gentle breeze
whistling through the palms and bamboo
giving voice to those in nature,
those who touch you.

Your life is, as with all God's creatures
small and light in the beginning,
growing in strength and stature
as the day passes.

Becoming at once all powerful
while starting your inevitable decline
into whispered death.

We are born
we grow
and we die.

Only through death
may we experience the opportunity
to live once again.

So it is with you,
So it is with us,
oh gentle breeze.

God's Many Ways

Debates rage
on and on
years, decades
centuries pass
Each side struggles
provincial need to be right
preparing them
for their next fight

East versus West
Buddha versus Christ
Muslim and Jew
Atheist, Agnostic
Wiccan too
Each has a personal stake
Each lives with a parochial view

Reincarnation for example,
there's a topic
intermittently hot
Eastern philosophy says
why yes, of course,
Christianity, no way
never, not!

Biblical scripture clearly states
for its readers to behold
"Man is slated but once to live"
and true as that recorded line may be,
does 'one lifetime' apply
to both body *and* soul?

If who we are
in reality is,
a cosmic energy
temporarily occupying
physical time and space
Is it not possible
a spirit filled soul
might acquire levels of learning
and opportunities to express,
experiencing truth and love
while on the way
to a place above
where streets are said
to be paved with gold?

Take for instance
one Christian scholarly belief
that the 'Angel of the Lord'
of Old Testament fame
is actually the Holy Spirit forerunner
of a different New Testament name

If that Old Testament Angel,
the singular one
sent by the Lord God
appeared at different times
in human form
before many and separate
Old Testament men,
returning each time as Holy Spirit
Was not that Spirit incarnate,
again and again?

Jumping ahead
a few thousand years
to a time of Empirical Rome's
persecution fears
A tribal people
inhabiting Canaan
one of their genealogical peers
put to death on the cross
representing humanity's temporary loss

Death on a cross
one man who did leave us
One believed in
and followed

His name was Jesus

Gone . . .
only then to return
once again
in body and soul,
as he was seen
for weeks on end
by followers both women and men
And then to leave them
He, heaven bound
once again

Jesus who lived
and died
As seen by the many
who testified
They had seen this
with their own eyes

As was recorded more than once
through Old Testament times
and into the New,
His Spirit incarnate
time and again
each time becoming
made into a man

And so today
this truth is believed
by Christian multitudes
of each and every nation

Explain please now
If you would,
the definition of reincarnation

Grave Situation

Lord give us strength
to go on one more day
that we might serve you
in some small way

Give us our bread
in a world that lacks
Give us a way
in your name to give back

The world today
has troubles its own
except for those
who through them have grown

The choices we make
the seeds of our struggles be
The decisions we take
can set us free
The choices each
ours to make
The risks of deciding
ours to take

Do Something
Do nothing
Do right
Do wrong
Moment by moment
Short life or long

Daily Choices, Decisions
of how we'll behave
follow or lead us
unto the grave

He Whom He Sent

It's finally come
we did wait and wait
Hell's half fury
unleashed at the gate
What now to do?
Wonder and Watch?
Or become involved
beyond the couch?

Who is right
Which can be wrong?
Only God knows
as He sits on His throne
King of all kings, Lord of all lords
At God's right hand
does He sit
God's own Son
'Son of Man'

Savior
Redeemer
Flesh of the One
Come to serve
the worst of us
that we might live
in His trust,
in His love
in His light
Through His Son
Through His own

He Whom He Sent
will carry me home.

Held

The one who fears death
has yet to grasp,
Belonging to the creator
is an eternal connection
of soul to Spirit
held tight from first to last

Physical realities held within
the realms of time and space
Existing that each being may grow
closer to God
and in its day
see His face

Birth relinquishes not
obligations
for each and every
sojourned soul
Neither through its liberation
nor material quest
To be held by the light of God
is eternal life
not eternal rest

Searching for identity
in times before
as now
Truths held out
for each to know
part and parcel
of moral indemnity

God's granted opportunities,
lessons and experience
reliant upon understanding of truth
Tests and trials
Choices between
self and unconditional love
by His living proof

Aligned betwixt
thought and breath
each mortal being must acquiesce
An eternal soul
held as example for us
by His truth
His love
His trust

Hook

Setting the hook
With each new cast
Dragline amidst the school
Same spot different bait
Different spot same bait
A repetitive trolling task

Each attempt
newly reborn
redaction refreshed
raucous, pious
Mausoleum arena
Hermitage publicly displayed

Fisher of men
tackle prepared
more or less than the one just past

In Peace

I harm me
to hurt you
Believing you'll notice
Thinking it matters
Hoping you'll come to the rescue

Your response
indifference,
a query of "what?"
"do you need something"?
'Yes' my mind whispers,
then shouts
'one moment of genuine concern'
like it once was,
in the beginning
when you cared,
or acted
perhaps, pretended?
as if you did

Not with the look
now given;
indignant
as if a bothersome flying insect
had invaded your space,
interrupting
and drawing your attention
away from all that is important to you,
anything
other than me

In retreat
I go to places of past
when I was alone,
without you,
and self-reliance
was the straw man
of my strength
who waited to laugh in my face
as I beat myself up, after

Desperately I sought you out
to take his place
and never have you disappointed
I harm myself
to hurt me,
to put an end to the pain
for I am invested, even less
than you are

Attempting to regain freedom
known only in the darkness
before the lightness of birth
and the weight of life

Longing for you to lash out
with finality
accomplishing that which I can't,
Release
once and for all
definitive separation
from man and God

to rest

In The Wake

We mourn not for the loss of life
but for the life that was
and is no more
The depth of our investiture
reminds us
of our own mortality
Our dear departed one
whispers to us
"Don't cry for me."

"We shall no longer share
a moment's experience together
until we meet once more
and you shall be guided
by blessing and spirit
into worlds unknown"

"Look each of you
at the collective gathered here
Mourn in my stead for each other,
for the one
into whose eyes you stare
at revealed fear and grief
masking personal disbelief"

We glimpse our own loss
A realization we encounter
at death's expense of another

For one day we too shall be gone
from this familiar place,
our little space
in this human race

And what are we racing to
or from?
Only the soul knows
the spirit's journey
along the path

It is our soul that mourns

Influences

Some say
it's DNA
Others claim
it's just the way
The way it is
from environs near and far
That makes us do
what we do
That make us who
we truly are

The way we're raised,
silver spoon
or rougher
often determines
how much we suffer

All come naked into the world
pure and virginal
caught up in the swirl
Of turmoil and trouble
none will escape
All will be pummeled
pounded and raped
Some raped of body
others of mind,
all beaten
all bruised,
different types
different kinds

And what can change
the way that we grow
What can remedy the ebb, the flow
of who we become
are
or will be
How are we ever
set totally free ?
From the dastardly things
we had to experience
as children, as youth
caught up in delirious
Ways of the world,
which torture and scour
our souls, our minds
each year, day and hour

Condemned to try
to live by umber and unction
in families
in groups
full of dysfunction

To where can we turn,
hide
or come forward
In what state of being,
courageous or coward

What is it that influences
above all others

Over siblings
fathers
even our mothers

Is it TV ?
Or money ?
Or jobs
we'd like to shove ?
No,
It's simply the abundance
or the lack
of love

Lahaina Town Crier

On the corner he stands
guitar slung,
like an outlaw's gun
First in one hand
and then the other,
the Book

He cries
He hollers
He sings
He laments
Addressing America
His pronouncement,
"Repent"

A neo John
A wilderness voice in paradise lost
Old Testament shame
New Testament cross

Icon tree behind
World around to bludgeon and blunt
Spectators and listeners abound
He,
a commercial affront

Frightened children cry
at his tantrum rant
Adults shriek
against incriminating words
which sting,
as they penetrate the skull
seeking a soft hollow, in each psyche

A knife in the heart
A spear to the lung
Silver bullet to the gut
fired from this,
Gospel hired gun

(Lahaina [pronounced, La High Na]
is a town on the west side of Maui)

Last Ride

Life in a world
of quasi vanity
Altered states
and relative sanity

How to fill
the void of time
on this lonesome trip
A stowaway's journey
in the grasp and hold
of this flesh and blood
tethered ship

Captain
of this small craft
Adrift,
No draft
for this lonely life raft

Cast ashore
on rock number three
Mind, soul, body
and me

Sailing vessels
moored and tied
their vast numbers still untold
Patiently awaiting appointed release
out with the ebb
in with the flow

Gliding as a vapor trail
above the rising tide
one last trip. .
this last journey. . .
my last voyage. . . .
life's last ride

O Lord

The nearer I draw to you O Lord
The closer I long to be
The more of you, You show me O Lord
The more I desire to see.

On My Knees

If I go to my knees Lord
Will it change my heart?
No

If I go to my knees Lord
Will it be a sign of reverence?
No

If I go to my knees Lord
Will it bring me closer to you?
No

If I go to my knees Lord
Will it exemplify my choice?
No

If I go to my knees Lord
Will it be proof of my desire?
No

If I go to my knees Lord
Will it bode of my devotion?
No

If I go to my knees
Will my action remind me;
You are Lord
and I am not?
Yes,
then the others will be true as well

Overweight

One hundred fifty plus pounds
of physical inertia
compresses claustrophobically
every segment of being,
snaring the spirit beneath
cutting off all routes of escape, save one
death

Only will liberation of the soul
allow the spirit
to regain its rightful place in the cosmos
awaiting rebirth
Until then,
the trap set
the quarry captured
soul and spirit smothered
beneath blood and flesh

Gagged by thoughts of here and now
Overwhelmed by outside influences
Keeping freedom held at bay
Cognition, light years distance away

Ignited by a spark of unconscious awareness
and fueled by inexplicable innate knowledge
of priori existential presence,
what once was
shall one day
be again

Parousia Timetable

Walking the plank
one of wormwood hewn
void of love
Alternating footfalls
some smooth
others rough

When will my time come
Father,
"Fear not my son,
soon enough"

Immersion into the abyss
of man and his makings
Watching hands grasp
all to be had
all to be taken
Fight or flight instincts
genetic predisposition of survival
What of their spiritual loss?
What of their souls' revival?

When will my time come
Father,
"Fear not my son,
soon enough"

Your presence arrives
from behind the blind spot
Yea, do emerge
Plant seeds of awareness
Seeds of light
within the darkened shroud
Seeds of acknowledgment
of eternal life
all to be sung aloud
Into hearts
hardened so tough

When will my time come
Father,
"Fear not my son,
soon enough"

Passion Soliloquy

Four comments from His lips
over less than one day's span
Tell of His conquest
over sin and death
showing us the way,
This Son of Man

His humanity spark
momentarily,
Asking if He must "take this cup"
cup of our responsibility,
Next thought
the Father's will
of His love
there is enough

Hanging up
looking down
Tilted heads skyward
eyes from the ground
"Forgive them Father,
they know not what they do"
Believing they silence me
Believing they follow you

This world's sin
is truly great
and of His being
did it satiate

Sin bearing down
a burden too great to carry
yet not one minute
did He tarry

As heavy a ransom
as there could be
"Why my God oh why
have you forsaken me?"
Not forsaken
now I see
though you've turned away

Clearly now
of this world's sin
not even a trace
shall transgress your face

For all who follow
and believe in me
there is eternal life
And to the faithful
of my words
certainly they will win it
Sins of all
now taken on
purpose and role fulfilled,
Finally, with one last breath,
"It is finished".

Patrician Prayer

Her spirit has flown
Eternal mystery now shown
The Savior's secret unsealed
His Redemption revealed

No longer alone
one of the world's disposable children
has now gone home

Known once only as words
through her ears were they heard
Alive now
within her soul's heart
Never again, shall she be apart
afar or removed
be it by crack or abyss,
from His love
from His eye
from His voice and caress

Death's design
to drown us
in sin's rising flood
Now crimson cleansed
her soul is saved
by the Lamb's precious blood

The pain
The shame
The world's bestowed guilt
Enough to choke
from heel
to hilt

Her temporal life
now for atoned
by Jesus the Christ
The Christian's way
to God's Holy throne

No longer in need
harm's way
or myopic blur
With open and loving arms
our Lord has received her

Patty now basks
in the light of the Lord
as she sings His praises
with heaven's angelic host
The almighty glories
of Father,
Son,
and Holy Ghost

Penance

She goes to her knees and feels helpless
The motivation heartfelt
The action embarrassing
Would that her desire be fulfilled
by this movement
yet in doing so she feels at once
guilt ridden,
so her shame keeps her seated
as conflict between her need to acquiesce
and her choice of not moving
keeps her farther from him

She remembers examples set forth
in words and pictures,
they spring to life
as two dimensional images
vivid in memory's mind
as if reality recalled

Taught the guidance reward
received by him
she too might share
a transcendent moment of peace,
yet still she sits
unable to reconcile mentally the emotion
whereby a similar action itself
condemns her sinfulness

The battle line drawn
between cognition and surrender
she realizes once again
his forgiving patience and understanding
Without a single word
nor one prepared
she kneels in prayer,
and he draws closer

Pilot

many days and nights have we traveled together
always have I relied upon you
for me, ne'er a care
with you at the controls

Warm and comforted have I been
no matter the weather
nor influences outside
while transported here and there
relaxed was I

all needs met
by your sanguinary blessed vessel,
announcing my presence
awaiting arrival
an appearance to be revealed

Scent of woman
Strength of man
these you gave
from the kiss of your breath
with the touch of your hand

no rejection
my election
Understanding your love accompanies me
as I follow the amniotic flood
of emotionally charge fluid
flowing before me

Still the Pilot
of my soul's heart
until the stain of mankind
blots and absorbs me
as part of the dark

Poison

Trials and Tribulations
Excuses and Lamentations
Peril and Consternation
Caution and Trepidation,
We all pick our poison

Painting ourselves into a corner
Soaring, clearing the bar
falling back to earth
with a bone shattering jar

Decisions and choices
we gladly make
oblivious to the possibilities
that within our ideals and desires are clothed
our near fatal mistakes

Our lives proceed
at our own intentional
break neck speed
With efforts to fill
each day, hour, minute
with as much fluff, flash and cash
as we can fit in it

Through our actions we've courted disaster
as the fickle finger of fate
takes aim directly at us
Whereby we throw the blame on others
in veiled attempts to keep our irresponsibility
covered, just enough

Believing once again
we've managed to avoid reciprocity
by keeping one step ahead
Until we discover
how far we can't run

We all pick our poison

Printed in Red

To your name I shriek
crying aloud,
please steal me away
from this madden crowd

Of all the books
upon which I have fed
it's your simple words
printed in red
That fills the longings
of my soul
That fills with love
my life's empty whole

The world I've known
takes care of me
keeps me chained
so fervently
keeps me fixated
upon its gold,
buys me
sells me
makes me grow old
It's your simple words
printed in red
That fills the emptiness
in my head

From here to there
and back again
slipping in and out
from sword to pen
Whom to trust
Whom to believe
They all speak
so eloquently

It's your simple words
printed in red and set apart
That fills the void
within my heart

This day they be friends
next generation foes
From this time to that
who really knows
Feed 'em
Fight 'em
Forget 'em

and so it goes,
and so it goes

My turning from your love
to Satan's graft
keeps my feet
upon this world's path

It's the merit of my actions
causing me this dread,
not your simple words
printed in red

Reclamation

Autumn falls away
as seasons change is marked
by winter's shorter days

Dark dank grey
billets the air
above snow's brilliant white
Sun gives way to moon
Days relent to night

So it goes
as nature sleeps
buried beneath the cold
And man remembers
God's promise and gift,
His advent
to reclaim the soul

~Season's Greetings

Religiosity

My mother hated being tardy for church
and each Sunday morning my brother she'd hurt
He would dawdle from room to room
and she would beat him
with her wooden spoon

Dragging him
out the door, across the yard
throwing him in the back of the car

the sting of weekly tears
made both our eyes wince,
he was four, I've not been inside
a single church since

Requiem Nails

There were two final nails
in the coffin of his marriage

The first when she informed him
to skulk as they ran,
so her boyfriend wouldn't see her
with him,
her husband

After that affair
he thought it couldn't get worse
that was until, the second
of course
It was then she told him
'her new friend' didn't believe in divorce

As a practicing Roman Catholic
he cared,
"That's nice" replied her husband
"apparently he has no problem
with an extramarital affair"

There were two final nails
in the coffin of his marriage

Rewards

Rewards, Rewards
held near and dear
rooted in the heart

Behind man-made excuses
and fault finding inquisition tours
the goals, the aims, the primary reasons
each religion has its start

Mohammed's sons' urges
seventy-two
nimble virgins

Siddhartha's quest
elevation
better, better, best

In Brahman's wake
a plethora of gods
to choose from for personal sake

For the Atheist
who cares?
everything is fake

Ah, the Christians
brandishing *the* word
all claimants to a Christ
The pharisaic dying daily in effigy
to prove themselves right

The carnal giving God the credit
for their abundant material prosperity
The third a relationship drawing nigh
admitting to a sinner's proclivity

Religious fodder for the struggles
of getting from here to there
but more profoundly, why
Psychological hankies
for each follower cries
a multitude of tears

For rewards do all expectantly look
hope for, gaze and pray
as the world's great religions
use shadowy smoke and mirrors
to hold tight in their grasp
disciples cowered in fear

the quintessential answer revealed;
a Trinity
no longer concealed
A spiritual treasure uncovered
the realized key of wealth
Belief in the heart
Father, Son and Spirit
are each greater than self

See Saw

how often is it
we turn to the Lord
with our hopes, our dreams
requesting aide and comfort
guidance and strength . . .

with a pinch
of favoritism,
reward
bringing to fruition
our self-centered need to serve
(whom?)
that God would know and understand
our desires,
are in His
best interest

Surrendering. . .
but not

Feeling abandoned
we turn from the Lord

Acquiescing
we will accomplish all
on our own!
and yet,
recognizing our inabilities
we flirt with the world
and its ways,
to obtain
that which we want
melded within private visions
of outcomes,
temptations

With veiled attempts
to be convinced
of the greater good
it represents . . .
to God
to Man,
yet always to ourselves

Convincing us of our need
believing the paramount pinnacles to be
grounded in linkage
to the prevaricated identity
we have broadcast. . .
from the mirror
to the world

State of Being

Unconditional love
is impossible for humans
From our first moment of existence
From our first breath
We live in a conditioned state of being

The closest we come
to experiencing God
is to serve the needs of others

Serving is never exclusively
ecumenical
parochial
evangelical
or dogmatic
It is seeing a need
and filling it compassionately
Recognizing a wrong
and righting it truthfully
Having love and sharing it honestly

Serving is love in action

Stewardship

For stewardship examples
to whom can we look?

To what policy
document
paper
or book?

Who can we follow
Who can we know

To guide our responsible service
As your Son always showed

He was from you
surely far above us

To whom can we turn
To whom can we trust?

Give us a common man
one of our own

Who has received your blessing
and represents your throne

That we might know
in some small part

The wisdom that comes
from a discerning heart

Let him show us
how to be strong

Have him teach us
between right and wrong.

We are no more than ordinary men
Selfish and ruthless corralled in pens

Pens of our own making
lusts and desires

Pens of our own illusions
with grandiose spires
Reaching to the heavens
we know it all,
just ask us.

His simple reply,
"Whoever can be trusted with little,
can be trusted with much."

Stream of Consciousness

Spark of energy entering a physical realm
At once becoming an "ism" of existence

Each macro and micro of its being
measured in 'time'
from nanoseconds to years
decades to centuries
Life force and perception choices
touch each grain of passing sand
which tumbles and slides unabated
through the hourglass
of each individual life span

Roles defined
Expectations sublime
Can all else be anything other than
exceptional disappointment

Where is release kept
How shall it be granted
At hand, Hope
always clinging
as if a dying vine
connected
only in form,
life
long ago gone

Across a once daunting threshold
of understanding
Safe, Saved
at last, all contacts
one by one abandoned

Each about their own being
with ne'er a thought of remembrance
beyond the marker,
the grave

Tempered Temptations

A weighted shard of ragged edged molten metal
The cast iron wedge of the world
is driven into the heart of the believer
with each compelling nuance
to become one with God

Peace disrupted
Satan's ranks laugh at our inept attempts
to declare allegiance to our Lord
They bow down to the one
who,
with a mere waggle of his finger
draws nigh those on the precipice point
balancing self and selfless

They laud his presence and persistence
knowing condemnation awaits
yet to bask momentarily with him
in his temporal glory
over one of God's own
is worth every minute of eternal damnation

How strong is such a force
that all material sins bend to honor him
and yet to do battle
on our own behalf
all we are given is free will to choose

The Box

An ancient box
once commissioned
to be constructed and suitable
Precise detailing
a dwelling place
to house
the uncontainable

Specific plans called for
nay, demanded
pure gold and acacia wood
with workmanship
to be the best
far beyond very good

When finished it would go
before its tribal followers
Declaring to a conflicted world
benefits of sin resistance
and the blessings of obedience

Containing selected items
special to Him for us
Evidence of His words and wishes
that merit all our trust

Somewhere along the way
from one era unto the next
this box was taken
stolen or lost,
it's unavailability to all mankind
an enormous mounting cost

After thirty-four hundred
or so odd years
eclipsing and passing on
Questions as to its whereabouts
No, its very existence
Be it known or be it shown
could settle many a score
would open many a door

Perhaps one day in the future
Exactly when still unknown
this daunting mystery
be solved and then,
evidence of His relationship sown

Where has the box been kept?
Where was it taken or sent?
When will it be revealed again?
This Ark of the Covenant

The Way

Service.
Now there's a word
many use and wear
readily proudly proclaimed,
their motivation
a discordant sense of duty
a cost of playing the game

Ask or not
they'll tell you why
the many ways it applies to them
followed by excruciating details
suffered and endured
along their path to martyrdom

Truth be told
reciprocity
is never far from their minds
it's the channel, the gauge
the measuring stick
protracting the distance
the twists, the bends
they're now willing to sojourn

While the only part
that comes from the heart
is how to receive
their self perceived
acceptable rate of return

The Word

Open my mind Lord
that i might know Your Word

Cleave the lobes and folds
as Abram did with his covenant sacrifice
that your spirit may pass between
these symbols of surrender

Live within my tissue and blood
as You did with Abraham
Wash clean with crimson Lord
the stain of gray
matters

Open my heart Lord
that i might learn Your Way

That your spirit would have a new place to dwell
joining together my existence
of the physical and spiritual
between this world and Yours

Open my eyes Lord
that i might see Your Truth

Make clearer
the distinction between self and righteous
As i look in the mirror
may Your Truth stare back
through these windows to the soul
Against the glare of the world

Open my arms Lord
that i might embrace Your being

Through the senses
Your presence
surrounds me
with all Your creations
Called to serve You Lord
I AM
guide

and be guided by
Thoughts of You

signs and markers
along the path,
stretch before
like a ribbon of fear
into the black
un-
known

as future

Up in Smoke

Chambered in the breach
waiting upon
the inevitable explosion
A chain reaction
set in motion
Ethereal now
caught up,
soaring
a burst of ignited emotion

Sparks of ingenuity
set free, released
psychic and physical realities
ablaze one moment
extinguished the next

And in between
Years of being,
known as life

Waiting Game
(not all who wander are lost)

I don't want to,
but I can
Do I have a choice?

Covenant made,
accepted
Impatience engaged

Faith in belief
Promise convened
tied to one, yet unseen

Comfort zone;
contentment
striving to understand
why the dreams, the visions?
if they're all out of our hands

The legwork;
joys and struggle
Experiences;
in a physical world
providing for self and others
as for God, for man

motivating words
innately felt or heard
keeping focus on,
or off?
as time slips away

victory;
here and now
blessings for only a few
preying on the rest
lifetime's taste and test?
nay,
a blink of the eye
for each and every lost soul
who wished, wondered, waited
while wandering astray

Within, Without

It is not the miles which separate us
for your very essence dwells by spirit
within
Connecting mind body and soul to you
daily

It is not the great distance of void
which comes between us
For as long as we have been
you preceded
Laying the foundation and groundwork
for our travels and paths

It is not the history or ages or numbers before
which cause our waiting
For you penetrate each minute particle
and atom of being

It is nothing we know or understand
which keeps us apart
It is our desire or disdain
for giving up a place for you
within our hearts

Worlds

This world is of merit,
of 'good and bad' works
The spiritual world
universally surrounding
beyond and above
is simply about
truth and love.

You of this world
so concerned
about you and you alone
in this time and place
And yet, when it involves
the hereafter
your obsession is
with everyone else,
where they may be
eternally,
and why.

Those of self righteousness
remove the blinders
from your eyes.

Focus on your relationship
with God
Let Him be concerned
with all the others.

For He loves them
as they are,
The same way He loves you,
as you are.

Worship Questions

Piously he sits
ears veiled by self-interest
Half heartedly he hears
listening to a sermon
filled with staccato words
of rapturous renouncing
and repetitious righteousness

As an elder
he is aware of Father's
exacting and eloquent
painstaking preparation
Collective words of God
indiscriminately spewed
to non-discerning ears
of parishioners
gathered in the pews

A sentence here
Another there
The making of aural contact
bobbing up for air
as if, a breath of cognition
overwhelms the flow
of disjointed admonitions
concerning man's sinfulness
and God's sanctity

As the pulpit voice drones on,
he stares lustfully
at the woman
seated across the aisle
wondering, can she be bedded?

Poised
Prim
and Proper,
Hands folded
resting on her Bible
the one auspiciously given,
a gift from her grandmother

Its weight cradled
between her thighs
as if hammocked
in the stretched wool
of her ankle-length skirt

The material forming a cot
upon which the words of God
wait,
always ready
to be unleashed

Without head movement
ever-so-slightly
her eyes stealthily glance
slowly to the right

As thoughts of transgressions
bathed in jealousy
and clothed in indignation
produce daggers
of envy's energy
longing to be propelled
at the target of her hatred

How dare she question my authority
as choir director
and my choice of Psalms?

Mental images trample
the young acolyte's efforts
to recall his cues and steps
A flood of remembered
sights and sounds
interrupts the concentration
of his pending duty bound
He turns to look at the mighty cross
festooned with the body of Jesus

If you love me God
why do you direct Father
to touch me,
with his fingers and his thing?

How can I serve you Lord
and serve them as well?
They are wolves
in sheep's clothing worn

Honoring you with false words
and claims
low these sixty minutes
While groveling in the dirt
and mired in the muck
until next Sunday morn

They heed not my words,
nor yours,
Nodding off
Looking around
Staring out the windows
each and every Sunday

Don't they know
I am speaking of you?
As I work hour upon hour
toiling at your task?
Don't they hear the lessons
of your people past?
Don't they care about their souls
I declare on your behalf?
I try to do your will
and still,
all they do is stray

I ask you to move upon their guilt
and make them give this day
With the pain of a scorpion's sting
to boost their meager offering

May they suffer
for turning from you
and your merciful grace
If they would but respond today
with a collection worthy
of a bountiful passed plate

(That I might use
the reserve this week
and never leave a trace)

Living on the island of Maui, Branch Isole
shares God's Word and Mana'o* in writing and
with individuals and groups visiting Hawaii.

Branch earned a Bachelor of Science teaching
degree at Texas State University, did post
graduate work at the University of Houston
and holds a Master of Arts in Theology
from Trinity Theological Seminary.

His catalogue of work includes poetry, short
stories and articles for journals, magazines,
newsletters and on the Internet at
www.manaopublishing.com

*Mana'o (pronounced Ma Na O)
is Hawaiian for Thoughts, Ideas and Opinions.

Other books by Branch Isole
available at www.manaopublishing.com

God. . .i believe ©
Simple Steps on the
Path of Spiritual Christianity ™
ISBN 0-9747692-0-7

Barking Geckos ©
Stories and Observations in Poetic Prose
ISBN 0-9747692-2-3

Seeds of Mana'o ©
Thoughts, Ideas & Opinions in Poetic Prose
ISBN 0-9747692-1-5

Reflections on Chrome ©
Parking Lot Confessions in Poetic Prose
ISBN 0-9747692-5-8

Postcards from the Line of Demarcation ©
Points of Separation in Poetic Prose
ISBN 0-9747692-6-6

Messages in a Bottle ©
Inspirations in Poetic Prose
ISBN 0-9747692-9-0

Saccharin and Plastic Band Aids ©
Comments in Poetic Prose
ISBN 0-9747692-8-2